Onion Man

Tightrope Books
17 Greyton Crescent
Toronto, Ontario
M6E 2G1 Canada
www.TightropeBooks.com

Edited by Shirarose Wilensky.
Cover design by Karen Correia Da Silva.
Illustration by David Poolman
Author photo David Poolman
Typesetting by David Bigham

This is a work of fiction. Any resemblance of characters to actual persons, living or dead, is purely coincidental.

 Canada Council   Conseil des Arts    ONTARIO ARTS COUNCIL
for the Arts   du Canada   CONSEIL DES ARTS DE L'ONTARIO

Produced with the support of the Canada Council for the Arts and the Ontario Arts Council.

Printed in Canada.

Library and Archives Canada Cataloguing in Publication

Mockler, Kathryn, 1971-
    Onion Man / Kathryn Mockler.

Poems.
ISBN 978-1-926639-39-0

    I. Title.

PS8626.O35O65 2011   C811'.6   C2011-902283-4

Kathryn Mockler

Onion Man

Onion Man

Clinton and I take off our
motorcycle helmets and
have a smoke before we
go in. Heat from the tarmac
rises like steam from coffee.
My feet burn from blisters,
from steel-toed boots. The
factory doors are as heavy
as the doors of Simpson-
Sears. The warm air makes
our skin damp, and it's as
hard to breathe in here
as it is in a bathroom after
a hot shower. We walk
past the Yugoslavian
women on the line who
wear white coats, plastic
gloves, hairnets. We make
sure our hard hats are in
place in case the foreman
sees us. We walk to the
warehouse—end of the line.
Only three women work
here: Clinton's mom on the
computer, Brenda in the
lab, and me. Clinton works
the Britestack, and I stand
across from him for ten
hours watching unlabelled
cans of corn. I make sure
each one is in place so he
can move them a thousand
at a time with a magnet, off
the conveyor belt, and down
to the forklift drivers. It is
so loud in here. Clinton and
I scream just to hear each
other. Half the time, I have
no idea what he is saying.

I punch us in while
Clinton puts our
lunches in the cool
room. The cool room
is a big room beside
the lunch area that's
as cold as a fridge
and that stays empty
during corn season.
Bud, the foreman,
lets us use it because
in terms of a lunch-
room the warehouse
workers get the shaft.
The rest of the factory
has a kitchen, fridge,
microwave, and four
vending machines
that we aren't allowed
to use because the
management doesn't
want us walking through
the factory. Bud made
a makeshift lunch area
consisting of two tables,
two vending machines,
and the cool room,
which I'm convinced
makes my sandwiches
taste like rubber.

There are four
big machines
in the warehouse.
Usually only
three are going
at a time. All I
know about the
process is what
I see here. The
cans come down
the conveyor
belt like stubby
tin soldiers and
march onto the
Britestack where
they form a square
of a thousand
cans. If they are
out of place or
fall down, I take
an L-shaped iron
rod to straighten
them up. That's
it. It's that boring.

The warehouse is better to work
in than the rest of the factory—
less pressure. My job may be
boring, but at least I don't have
any responsibility. My job isn't
important. Clinton's is, but I
wouldn't want his job for any-
thing. I don't have to worry
though—they never let women
run the big machines. Working
in the lab would be good. The
room is tiny and soundproof,
and they have a little fan going
and a radio. I peeked in the lab
a couple of days ago. Brenda
offered me corn to eat right
out of the can, and I did, and
it tasted really good. I've never
eaten canned corn before. My
mother always buys frozen,
but now I think canned tastes
better. It's sweeter and has a
better consistency. I ate it cold
but imagine it's good warm
with butter and salt and pepper.
Clinton says you can buy a case
wholesale from the factory for
ten bucks. Maybe I'll do that.

The lights and no
windows trick me
into thinking it's
day. Except when
I take my break
and slip out the
side door for a
cigarette. The air
is cool compared
to the air inside.
The sky is clear
because we're
outside city limits,
and there are no
clouds, few lights.
I hear crickets the
way I imagine my
mother did growing
up on my grand-
parents' dairy farm.
Corncobs are piled
in pyramids ready
to be husked, de-
cobbed, and sealed
in cans. Before we
leave tonight, Clinton
and I will stash an
A&P bag full of
fresh corn to eat
when we get home.
We'll have garlic
bread with cheese
and fall asleep
in front of the TV
—the window fan
blowing our hair on
and off our faces
like wind and weeds.

———

On my first day
I walked through
the factory without
my hardhat: Bud
Richards hollered
at me in front of
everybody. Now I
never forget. —It
seems like Bud
always picks on
me, I say to Clinton.
—It's because you
work in the ware-
house, Clinton says.
Bud's old school; he
thinks only men
should work here.

————

Clinton and I first met
at a bar downtown called
Key West where it's
easy to get in with a fake
ID. I was at the back
with my friends. Clinton
had a black marker he
used for graffiti. Without
asking, he sat down beside
me and wrote his name
on the knee of my jeans.

We have
five minutes
before our
shift starts.
We get pop
from the
vending
machine
and then
sneak off
to the stacks
to share
a cigarette.
There are
so many
crates, and
they are
stacked
so high, it's
overwhelming.
Each crate
holds a
thousand
cans, and
they're stacked
almost to
the ceiling.
They're as
high up
as trees, as
telephone
poles, as
some office
buildings
downtown.
If I wanted
to, I couldn't
count them.
Being in
the heart

of the stacks
is like being
in a maze.
It's where
the forklift
drivers
smoke up,
take turns
taking naps.
And they
won't get
caught;
no one
goes back
there—not
even Bud.

Clinton hates
books and teachers.
The only book
he thinks is
worth reading
is *Beautiful Losers*
because he knows
they'd never teach it
in high school.

Clinton doesn't look at me
when we work. He looks
down at the drivers or off
into space. I think about my
grandfather—how he doesn't
remember what I look like
but knows my name. And
my grandmother, she cries
a lot—not in front of me,
but I know she does. I think
about my mother and how
she went to university,
came out with a C-average
but could get any job she
wanted—how slowly her
skin is turning yellow, how
her hands shake all the time.
All she likes to do is sleep.
The cans are as shiny as
nickels. I count them to stop
myself from thinking. Maybe
that's what Clinton does.

In the last week of classes, Clinton almost got himself suspended for telling his English teacher to fuck off. They gave him his grade twelve diploma but said he wasn't welcome back for grade thirteen. It was the vice-principal who said it, the one with the shrivelled arm from polio. He was the same guy who gave me a hard time in grade nine and ten but was nice when I stopped skipping school. Clinton said in BC they don't have grade thirteen, so we're as good as graduated. Then he pinned me on the bed, and he wouldn't let me up until I said I'd move there.

———

There's been a gas leak and we're all
outside on the grass. It was a close
call. If one person had lit a cigarette,
the whole place would have blown
up. We're not supposed to smoke
inside, but we all do anyway. My
hard hat is upside-down on the
ground, rocking from the wind. I'm
picking blades of grass, biting the
bitter white ends between my teeth.
Clinton is lying on his back, smoking,
hand beneath his head, eyes shut. It's
only seven o'clock, still light out. I'm
hoping we'll be let go for the night,
then we can rent a movie or something.

After my dad left my mom
because he was having an
affair, I slept in my mother's
room every night until I was
five. There are two things
I believe to be true but that
I know could not have
happened. The first is the
face of a black wolf looking
at me through the window
beside my mother's bed on
the side where I slept; the
second is the devil, masking
as a little boy with freckles,
sleeping in my mother's
closet with the door shut.
Every night I lay frozen
in fear of these two things
—neither of which I had
bothered to look for, yet I
was certain both were there.

They've just moved my
grandfather from the
Chelsey Park nursing
home to the Alzheimer's
ward at the London
Psychiatric Hospital.
My grandmother is very
annoyed because it's only
been a few days and they
have already lost two of
his good shirts. Clinton's
with me for the visit.
Most of the patients are
strapped to chairs, their
arms are long and thin
like sagging branches.
My grandfather's in bed
in a hospital gown. He
talks gibberish, doesn't
know who the hell I am.
My grandmother told
me to bring my grand-
father chocolate. When
I put it in his mouth, he
spits it right back out.

Clinton says that if he
got sick like my grand-
father where he couldn't
remember anything
about his life or anyone
he used to know, he'd
have killed himself by
now. I ask him how he
would do it, and he says
he's not sure. —I'd take
sleeping pills, I say.
—Pills are no good, he
says. If they don't do
the job right, you might
wake up retarded.

One-by-one
the women
on the line
shuck corn.
Hairnets and
white coats
make them
clinical and
sanitary like
they are out
of a dream, a
sci-fi movie.
It is so hot in
here, I don't
know how
they stand to
wear those
coats. As I
walk past
them on my
way to the
warehouse, I
can't help but
feel superior.

———

Now that
I work the
night shift
I have no
idea what
my mother
does in the
evenings or
how drunk
she gets.

There's a man who sits
at the lunch table by
himself. Every night he
peels an onion and eats
it as if it were an apple.
I eat with Clinton and
his mom. I usually bring
a cheese sandwich and
a banana from home.
Sometimes we order
pizza. Lately, I've been
buying Lifesavers after
lunch, eating them until
my teeth are coated in
sugar, my tongue numb.
I think I have a canker
but keep doing it because
I like to time how long
a single candy takes to
dissolve in my mouth.
One pack usually lasts
two hours of my shift.

Stacey strips at the Red Lion on
weekends. We went for a beer
at the Brunswick, met a guy
who's a friend of a friend of a
guy who works at the factory.
He asked for my phone number;
I gave it. Clinton doesn't under-
stand why, on my night off, I
don't want to spend it with him.

Every day after school Clinton and I
went to the London Chinese Café,
but since we started working at the
factory this summer we haven't been
once. It's the type of place old men
go to smoke and drink coffee in red
vinyl booths. I have never ordered
Chinese food at the London Chinese
Café. Clinton has ordered chicken
balls before, but I usually get grilled
cheese. The owner's name is Wanda,
and she doesn't like it when students
stay for a long time and drink coffee,
if it's busy. If it's not busy, you can
stay as long as you want, and she'll
keep filling up your coffee cup until
you feel guilty and order some fries.
During the school year, when the
three high schools—Central, CCH,
and Beal—get out in the afternoon,
it's filled with punks and skinheads.
Sometimes the skinheads are the racist
kind, sometimes not. It all depends
on the colour of their boots and laces.
It's best, in any case, not to look them
in the eye. Once, in the smoking pit, a
skinhead called Clinton a fag just for
looking at him and said he was going
to beat him up, but then the bell rang
and everyone from the pit threw away
their cigarettes and went inside for
class. Clinton had art and was getting
critiqued on a painting he did of a Joy
Division album cover. I had history,
and we were watching a film about
WWII and the concentration camps.

I got the job through Clinton's mom who works at the factory during corn season. Last summer Clinton worked here, and this summer he suggested I work here too so we can make money faster to go out west. Since he bought his motorcycle in April, all Clinton can think about is leaving London. He craves the mountains the way some people crave chocolate. He wants to drive across the country on his Harley. I'm not sure it's safe. I think the bike will break down along the way, and I'm afraid we'll be eaten by bears.

My grandmother
says I'll never be
a farmer's wife
unless I can cut the
head off a chicken.
I don't want to be a
farmer's wife or
kill any chickens.

There's a hum in
the air that puts
me into a trance
every time I walk
through the factory.
It's like the hum
transforms me into
a different person,
into the person I
have to be at work.
I'm quiet here, more
subdued. I conform
because everyone
else conforms. If
Clinton's mom hadn't
gotten me the job,
I wouldn't have
lasted a day. I know
this, and Clinton
knows it too.

Me, Clinton, and Stacey
drop a hit of acid each,
hang out in the food court
at the Galleria. When the
security guards kick us
out because the mall is
closing, we go to Harris
Park where we find
boxes of creamers, left-
over from a free concert.
We stomp on the thimble-
shaped containers until
our shoes, socks, pants,
shirts are covered in
cream. We laugh to the
point of gagging. Stacey
is thirsty, drinks the
creamers one-by-one. She
squirts a creamer in my
face and says it looks like
cum. A cop car pulls up.
We run down to the river,
lie beside the water on
our backs in damp grass.
Stacey tells us about being
molested, and Clinton
comforts her in a way
that makes me tense. Then
he tells a story about his
dad, a belt, his sister, and
blood. And the stories
meld into each other like
rainwater and dirt. They
are bonding, but I don't
share anything about my-
self, although these two
know more about me than
anyone. The words *nervous
Jesus* repeat in my mind.
This high won't go away;
acid's just not fun anymore.

The onion man wears
pressed practical clothes
that will last; they will
likely outlast us all.

I ask my mom
why so many
immigrants at
the factory are
from Yugoslavia.
I don't know
because I don't
watch the news.
But she reads
the *London Free
Press* every night
in her yellow
armchair, smoking
Matinee Extra
Milds, drinking
caffeine-free
Diet Coke that
is more often
than not vodka-
laced. She says
there's social
unrest there, and
they're probably
refugees. I hear
a slur that gets
me off the couch
to sniff her glass,
and she lets me.

———

When he was picking
up smokes at the store,
Clinton saw his math
teacher, the one who
failed him twice in
grade ten general math.
—I have a tremendous
urge to kill my teacher,
he says as he kicks the
stand on his bike. —So
do it. I'm not stopping
you. I'm joking, but
something in his tone
makes me feel he's not.

—

Clinton thinks
that working
is better than
being in high
school. I don't
agree at all,
but if I tell him
I don't mind
high school,
he'll think I'm
conforming.

When we pass the administration
office, the girl behind the front
desk calls out to me. —You have
to wear this, she says, hands me a
white cotton coat with snap buttons.
—Why? I ask. —All women have
to wear them, she says. —But I'm
not on the line, I say. I just work
in the warehouse. —Doesn't matter,
she says. Bud saw you without it
and gave me shit. —What an ass-
hole, I say. The girl returns to her
desk as I slip into the coat. It is
heavy. It is two sizes too big. I hold
up my arms, pretend I'm drowning.

In the stacks, Clinton pulls
me toward him, tries to kiss
me, grab my tits. When I
say stop, he says, —You're
frigid. —I don't like being
grabbed at, I say. —I wasn't
grabbing, he says. I was
being affectionate. He opens
the first two snap buttons on
my white coat, pulls me
close. —That coat is kind
of sexy, he says. It makes
you look like an immigrant.

Clinton's dad married his
mom after she got pregnant
in high school. What they
said about me was—they
didn't want Clinton to make
the exact same mistake.

Tony's the guy who gives me
breaks. He has just walked
me to the nurse; I can't breathe
in there. The nurse is listening
to the radio and humming a
Michael Jackson song while
taking my temperature with
an electric thermometer. Her
hands are pudgy and soft, and
she does everything slow. She
says I'm fine but can go home
if I want, and I do. I call my
mother. And when I hear her
slurred voice answer the
phone, I hang up. I take a cab
all the way into the city, and
it ends up costing thirty bucks.

The first night, time went
by fast because it was new,
but since then, the hours
drag on the way I imagine
seconds do for kittens
drowning in a burlap bag.
When I'm at the factory
everything feels as if it's
in slow motion, but when
I'm off work time moves
like quicksand. I don't get
to sleep long enough or
watch TV long enough or
stay long enough at the bar.
All the things I like to do
become memories before
I've had enough time to
experience them. At least
Clinton gets to do some-
thing with his hands. There
are times an hour goes by
and I won't have picked up
the iron rod once. Tonight
I'm thinking of ways to
make the job less boring.
Tomorrow I'm gonna sneak
in my Walkman, or a book.
I don't want to complain or
ask for another job because
Bud could give me a job
that's much worse. And the
one good thing is—me and
Clinton get the same breaks.

Clinton thinks
I think I'm
too good to
work at the
factory. He
says I'm a
snob because
my mother is
a snob, even
though we're
not rich. He
thinks it's
because I've
grown up
around rich
people in
North London.
When I tell
him I hate
rich people,
he says, —It
doesn't
matter cuz
you act like one.

I tell Clinton
I'm going
on a diet
which means
I can't
eat junk
food or
any chips
anymore. He
looks at me
and says,
— You're
not fat, but
you're not
skinny either.

My father and
I have an
arrangement—
he doesn't
want to see
me, and I don't
want to see
him. The last
memory I have
of him living
with us is
a fight in
which a beer
bottle was
thrown like
a fastball
at the wall
beside my
mother's
face and I was
hiding under
a table saying,
—Don't hurt
her, don't you
hurt her, under
my breath.
It's hard to
love someone
who makes
you this afraid.

———

The guy from the bar
never called. I didn't
expect him to but was
afraid he might when
Clinton was around. I
saw him the other day
at the market. His father
owns the butcher shop,
and that's where he
works on the weekends.
He waved as I walked
by, and I pretended that
I didn't see the raw
hamburger in his hands.

We got the night off because
they ran out of corn. They didn't
tell us until the last minute.

———

Clinton says if I
went to a movie
without him and
met a guy like
Stacey did, he'd
die. And if I ever
did things behind
his back that he
didn't know about,
he says he would
have to kill someone.

I climb onto the machine, take my
Walkman out of my blue canvas
army bag. Just as I'm about to blast
the volume on my *Meat is Murder*
tape, Bud walks by. —If you even
think about listening to that thing,
you can kiss it goodbye. I am high
enough up that I could spit on him
and I want nothing else at this
moment then to do just that. My
face is burning, and I'm so mad I
feel like crying. I look over at
Clinton who is giving me an I-told-
you-so face. It's lucky we can't
talk to each other on the machines
or else I'd tell him to fuck right off.

This morning
we had what
Clinton likes
to call a wake-
and-bake. I
don't like that
name because
it makes us
sound like
we're stoners.

———

Clinton comes up behind me and starts
tickling. I want to be annoyed with him
but can't help laughing. He chases me
out of the stacks giggling until I come
face-to-face with Bud, who looks down
at me sternly, his white hard hat tucked
neatly under his arm. The foremen wear
white hats and the workers wear baby
blue. I would like to remind him that he's
breaking safety regulations, but I wouldn't
dare. Bud says, —We're not paying you
to fool around. Clinton nods and salutes
him. I don't understand why he isn't scared
of Bud. —He's just a person, Clinton says.
Besides, I know he really likes my mom.
—He's mean, I say. Clinton shrugs —So
he's mean, you still get paid, don't you?

I ask my mother if I can
start a compost in the
backyard. She says, —Don't
do anything smelly back
there, don't do anything
that will attract raccoons.
I ask her if she is at all
concerned about acid rain
or air pollution because
in twenty years time we
won't be able to breathe.
—Don't worry, she says
The government will do
something before things
get really out of control.

———

Sometimes Clinton
drives the motorcycle
so fast I can't catch
my breath. He knows
it scares me but keeps
doing it, especially
if we've just had a
fight. If I remember
to keep my mouth
closed and to breathe
out my nose, it helps.
Sometimes I think, I
could die right now.
One wrong move and
we'd both be dead in
a second, and it wouldn't
matter. I can feel the
hair at the back of my
helmet, blowing. I
like the way that must
look from the street.

The man who eats onions
has missed six days in a
row, and no one but me
has noticed. He's the type
of man who could boast
forty years of working,
not a sick day in his life.
Someone must be dead.
Maybe it's his wife who,
I imagine, has thick arms
with which she lays down
layers of cool white sheets
and packs an onion in his
lunch box every single day.

Clinton let five thousand cans fall
twelve feet and Bud's on the floor
yelling, —What are you blind or
something? I'm standing with my
hands over my mouth listening to
the noise of the factory to block
out Clinton's embarrassment. Even
the forklift drivers are pitching in.
We are all using our lunch break
to clear the cans from the floor,
throwing the dented ones into a
wood crate. Bud Richards is sixty.
Drum tobacco sticks out of the
pocket of his white shirt, and so
does a pen with a silver clip. When
he yells, his face turns red, and he
yells the way I imagine he yells at
his wife at the supper table. Clinton's
stoned; I'm the only one who knows.

———

Some
people
wear ear
plugs
in the
factory
because
of the
noise. I
don't and
Clinton
doesn't.
But I've
noticed
lately that
I'm not
hearing
him as
well as I
used to.

We've worked fifteen days
in a row. Today we called
in sick. I called first, then
Clinton called and said he
had diarrhea. I had to leave
the room just to keep from
laughing. It's three o'clock
in the afternoon and so
humid it feels like a lead
weight has been placed on
my chest. My mother is at
work, and Clinton's mad
because I won't have sex.

The forklift drivers
told Clinton he
should dump me
and go out with
someone from the
factory. When I ask
why, he says so he
can get laid more
often. Clinton says
he told them he
couldn't do that
because he has to
love someone first.

We're not
unionized
and only
get paid
six dollars
and fifty
cents an
hour. The
forklift
drivers and
anyone who
was with
Green Giant
before they
switched
to Pillsbury
gets twenty.

Last night there were tornado warnings
and the power went out. My mother
made us go to the basement with flash-
lights and water and crouch behind the
stairs where no windows could burst
and cut us with shards of glass. My
mother said we had to take this seriously
because London is in the southwestern
Ontario tornado belt. So we sat on green
garbage bags she had filled years ago
with empty vodka bottles and moth-
infested clothes and had never bothered
to throw out. We listened to the radio
on my Walkman for two hours before
going back up. In the end, there wasn't
any storm, just the worry and the threat.

———

It's been two weeks, and
I just found out from one
of the forklift drivers that I
was right. Someone did
die, but it wasn't the onion
man's wife—it was his son.
He wrapped his car around
a tree. That's the way he
described it: wrapped around
a tree as if it were a present.

I'm reading on the job
even though I'm not
supposed to. To get
my attention, Clinton
throws a lighter at
the steel rail beside
me. All the cans are
starting to back up.
I take my long metal
hook and try to shift
them into place. The
ones at the back won't
straighten out, and it's
fucking things up all
the way down the line.

The guy who
works with
Clinton's mom
on the computer
who we call
"Egg" behind
his back is off
sick for the next
few days, so
they're sticking
me on there.
I don't know
how to use
a computer.
What if I break
it? What if I
fuck it up?

I bumped into Steve from the bar
on Richmond Street just in front
of the Selby Building. I didn't notice
before that he had so many freckles.
He said he had wanted to call, but
someone told him I had a boyfriend.

The first time Clinton and I had
sex was the same night my mother
was admitted to the psych ward.
We weren't sure what she was on,
but she was hallucinating snakes
and spiders. I called 911. Clinton
thought it was Valium, but I just
thought that she was really really
drunk. Clinton slept over that
night; we fucked on my bed. I
didn't bleed; I didn't get pregnant.

———

Once when we were
having a fight, Clinton
said fucking me was
like fucking a brick
wall. —You just lay
there. You don't do
anything. He likes to
try and hurt me, and it
makes him angry when
I act like I don't care.

It's 2:00 a.m.
Clinton and I
are staying up
so he can tape
Skinny Puppy
on *Brave
New Waves*.

When I touch
the walls of
the factory,
they vibrate
and I finally
feel a part of
things. Once
Clinton caught
me just as we
were leaving
the building.
He looked at
me but didn't
say anything.
When Clinton
and I first went
out he used to
watch me all
the time. Even
if I couldn't
see his eyes,
I felt him
watching me,
the way I ate
and read and
watched TV.
I felt it the
way a sleeping
person feels
a blanket
placed over
them by some-
one they love.

Every night the
same rumour—
we're getting off
early. And it's
never true.
Clinton thinks
the management
is spreading it on
purpose to make
us work harder.

Clinton says that if he has
to stay in London any longer,
he will take a gun and shoot
himself without hesitation.
—Some people like London,
I say. Some people think it's
a nice place to live. —Like
who? he asks. —Like
immigrants, I say. —I bet if
they were born here they
wouldn't. I bet they'd think
it was just another shitty town

It's the end of our
shift and Clinton
and I are stealing
cobs of corn from
the pile outside.
Sweat is dripping
from Clinton's
forehead into his
eyes. The handle
of the plastic bag
is digging into my
hand, and I will
have to ride all the
way home like this.

———

After the night shift I like the
sky best just before it becomes
day when it's as blue as the
glow of a TV in a dark room.
Sometimes when Clinton
falls asleep before me, I sit
on the front porch and watch
the sky lighten with a pack of
cigarettes, a bottle of pop.
Everything is damp and warm
except my legs, which are cool
from air conditioning. This is
the only time I don't think
about the factory or Clinton.

My mother and I just
got into a fight because
she doesn't think the
brand of cigarettes
I'm smoking is feminine
enough. —Player's is
for men, she says, and
Matinee and Craven A
and Du Maurier are
more feminine to smoke.

Everyone
avoids
the onion
man more
than they
did before.
I do it too,
and it's
getting so
I can't
look at him,
so I can't
stand him
because I
just end
up feeling
guilty.

Watching *The Nature of Things* is
making me suicidal. Our shift got
cancelled tonight because there's
no corn, but I can't get out of bed
because I watched a program about
the destruction of the Amazon rain-
forest. I ask my mother how she can
live life while something like this is
going on. She says maybe I can get
a job doing something about it when
I'm older. —One person can't do a
thing, I say. The world's fucked up;
and no one is paying any attention.

Clinton and I were dating for two years before I let him into my mother's room. Even though the rest of the house is clean because she has a cleaning lady, no one goes in there. Her room is piled with old magazines and clothes and papers and cigarette packs and empty vodka bottles and shoes and purses and God knows what else. Every once in awhile she makes an attempt at cleaning it, but it never lasts. Because her bedroom is off of the living room, I always worry one of my friends will open the door by accident. It looks like the room of a bum. And it smells in there too. When Clinton saw her room for the first time, he was in a state of shock. At his house, everything is tidy. If it were up to me, I'd take a shovel, throw it all out. She won't let me because she says there are important things in there; only she knows where it goes, where it all is.

In the parking lot on
our way home, two
workers are fighting.
They yell and swear
then break out in
fisticuffs. Tony turns
to Clinton and laughs.
—They're fighting
over a girl, he says.
Everybody walks by.
No one breaks it up.
Everyone is tired or
high or drunk and
wants to go to sleep.
As I get on the back
of the bike, I see one
of the men pull
something out of
his pocket and whip
it at the other. It's
pink. It's a toy. It's
a pink stuffed elephant.
—People here are
rough, I say to Clinton.
—No they aren't, he
says. They're normal.

Egg has returned, so I'm back on the Britestack. I think I liked the computer job better. Using the computer wasn't as scary as I thought it would be and wasn't as mind-numbing as this job. Also, I got to talk to Brenda while she tested the corn.

—

What difference
does it make
what kind of
cigarettes I
smoke? They
all give you
cancer anyway.

Clinton's tools are lined
up on the sidewalk like
knives. We're now a half-
hour late for work. The
Italian man who lives next
door has offered to help.
He used to own a bicycle
shop on Richmond Row.
I'm on the front steps,
smoking, while they kneel
over the bike with the
concentration of surgeons,
jeans and hands stained
with oil instead of blood.
We've never been this late
before, and I don't want to be
the one that has to call in.

———

My grandfather caught pneumonia
for the third time this year. No one
can believe the strength of his
constitution. Because death would
be the best thing—like a wounded
bird found at the side of the road,
whose neck, in an attempt to end all
suffering, must be broken—my
grandmother's signing a form. The
next time he gets sick, the doctors
won't treat him with antibiotics but
will just give him something for pain.

It takes about forty-five minutes
by motorcycle to get from
London to Grand Bend. I sit on
the back of the bike for so long
my bum hurts, and we can't talk
because the wind makes it too
hard to hear. On the way there,
I think about how Clinton says
there are helmets with radios
and some that have headphones
you can plug a Walkman into

The patio at the Brunswick faces
Tim Hortons and the Greyhound
station. The band inside is so
loud the whole bar shakes. The
music, especially the drums,
bounces off the bus station
windows. It sounds like the band
is playing there instead of inside
the bar. On weekend nights a
regular in a white apron barbeques
hotdogs and holds the buns with
hands you know he forgot to wash
when he used the bathroom. Clinton
and I used to come here underage.
Clinton grew a beard so that he
wouldn't get carded. I wore makeup.

Lately some
of the drivers
have been
getting high
and stealing
the onion
from the onion
man's lunch.
They laugh
when he opens
his lunch box
and it isn't
there. I don't
know how
he can stand
it. I think
Clinton might
have been in
on it once,
but he won't
tell me if he's
the one who
had the onion.

Last night Bud
handed me a
broom and said
I had to sweep
the entire factory
for the length
of my shift. Ten
hours. Although
it's boring, I like
this job because
I'm left to my
own devices. I can
read, sleep, and
listen to music
without worrying
about Bud yelling
at me. Being on
the machines has
more status than
sweeping the floor.
Clinton thinks I've
been demoted. But
if I like it, and
there's no change
in pay, how can
it be a demotion?

The other day one
of the forklift drivers
asked me if Clinton
could get him some
weed. When I ask
Clinton if he's selling
drugs at the factory,
he says, —Just hash
and pot. When I first
met Clinton, he didn't
smoke or do drugs or
hardly drink. I got him
into all that stuff, and
it's making me think
I'm a bad influence.

Now that I sweep
the floor, I get
the same breaks
as the onion
man who sweeps
the other side
of the warehouse.
On break, he sits
at one end of the
table and I sit at
the other. I try to
smile and make
eye contact, but
he just looks away
and pretends I'm
not there. He's in
a country where
he doesn't speak
the language. No
one is befriending
him. I wonder if
he's lonely. I
wonder what he
thinks about.
When I mention
this to Clinton,
he says,—Worry
about yourself.

The first time Clinton and I went out we walked on train tracks near his parents' house. When a train came, Clinton put a quarter on the track, and we waited until it came back flat. I used to do the exact same thing with my grandfather, only he used a penny.

There was a pregnancy scare. Even my
mother noticed I hadn't had my period
in awhile. After she was drunk enough,
she got the nerve and said, —Don't ruin
your life. In the morning, we'll make
an appointment at the clinic. But in the
morning, I told her I got my period. I
told her I was so relieved, that I would
never be careless again. I told her I'd
learned my lesson. Every time I went
to the bathroom, I put tampon wrappers
in the wastebasket to keep up the ruse
even though I was really starting to get
worried. I got Stacey to pick me up a
pregnancy test at the drugstore, which
I've done for her twice before. When
she gave me the test, I was too scared
to pee on the stick and just stared at the
box instead. I kept the box in my closet,
hidden under my public school diaries.
Two days later I got my period. Once
the scare was over, I asked Clinton
what we would do if I got knocked up.
He said he'd work at the factory, and
I'd stay home with the kid. —What
about an abortion? I asked. —Abortions
are for one-night stands, he said, and
for people who don't love each other.

When my
mother
was drunk
she said
motherhood
enslaves
women.

It made
me think
she didn't
want me;
it made
me not
want to
be a
mother.

Two women from my mother's work
phone me when she's not home. They
say they know she's drinking again
because she calls in sick a lot and
shows up late for work. I'm afraid she's
gonna be fired, but they say they want
me to be part of an intervention. I don't
want to but, apparently, without me,
it just won't have enough of an effect.

We stole a case of canned
corn and tied it to the back
of the bike with bungee
cord. You'd think we'd be
sick of it by now, but we're
not. Tony is driving beside
us in a white van. At the
stoplight, I wave; Clinton
gives him the finger. The
light turns green, and
Clinton wants to show off,
wants to show his bike
can go faster than a stupid
white van. He takes off too
quickly, the bike bucks
like a bull, we get thrown
onto the road. The cans of
corn crush and burst open.
Kernels spill around us like
loose change. Clinton rolls
the bike off the road while
Tony kicks the cans to the
curb so other cars can pass.
My arm's cut and so is my
knee. I can't feel any pain
because everything is numb.
The streetlights are bright,
and my hands are shaking
the way I've seen my grand-
father's hands shake, my
mother's hands shake.
When we pile into the van,
Clinton says something's
wrong with his head. I'm
too out of it to be worried.

At the hospital, we call my
mother. She's probably
passed out, and that's why
she's not answering the
phone. We're not hurt bad,
and nothing's wrong with
Clinton's head—just shock.
I have a swollen hand they
say isn't broken or sprained.
My knee is scraped up, but
I don't want them to touch
it. Bits of dirt and gravel are
ground into the skin. The
nurse says if my knee isn't
cleaned, it'll scab over, and
the grit will embed in my
flesh like twigs in cement.
—Besides, she says, you could
get an infection. She wants
us both to get a tetanus,
which is good for ten years.
She's scared me enough so I
get mine, but Clinton refuses.

Clinton's mom has been
driving us to the factory
in her convertible. It's
going to cost over two
thousand bucks to fix
the bike. Clinton intends
on doing it himself and
just paying for the parts.

———

Clinton's mom will be here
in an hour to pick me up
for work. To relax, I go
into the bathroom, splash
cold water on my face. My
mother knocks, says *hurry*
because she really has to
go. I don't know why, but
suddenly I could throw
something. I could break
the mirror. I could tear the
doors off the cabinet, and I
know it would feel great.
I open the door and let her
in. As I walk to the kitchen,
I hear her farting, notice the
bathroom door ajar, slam it
and yell, —Shut the fucking
door when you take a shit.

At his parent's house for dinner,
Clinton's father asks me what I
plan to do next year. I tell him
my mother wants me to go to
university, so I have to do grade
thirteen. His father asks me what
I would take in university, and
I say English. He asks what I
would do for a job with English,
and I say I have no idea —What
about our plans for BC? Clinton
says. —I don't know. I didn't mean
for it to come out like that, it just
did. I had a plan and didn't even
know it. There's a long pause; and
the rest of dinner is pretty tense.

The onion man
is regal the way
he sits at the
lunch table. I bet
he used to be a
business owner.
Imagine owning
your own business
then giving it up
so you don't get
killed. But his
son died anyway.

My mother's co-worker calls me when my mother
is at work, says she's coming over to search her
bedroom for drugs before the intervention. I tell
her she doesn't need to because my mother doesn't
do drugs, she just drinks like a gutter fish. I laugh,
but her co-worker doesn't laugh. She doesn't believe
me, so I tell her, —I'll do it, I'll check out her room,
I'll be thorough. But she says sometimes when we
love someone, we only see what we want to. The co-
worker will be here in half an hour. My mother's
room hasn't been cleaned in ten years, and there's
shit all over the place. Even though she doesn't
deserve it, I get a bunch of green garbage bags and
start stuffing them. I mix the bottles with clothes
and shoes so they won't clink and drag the bags
to the basement. In all, I stuff ten bags full in fifteen
minutes. Then I run the vacuum over the floor, but it
hardly even picks up the dirt. When the co-worker
arrives she's shocked by the filth of my mother's
room, even after I've cleaned it. She looks through
my mother's drawers and finds an old bottle of
Valium, which she wants to take to the intervention
for evidence. Even though I don't think it's the right
thing to do because it's an invasion of my mother's
privacy, I let her take the empty bottle with her.
What I feel for her isn't love—more like obligation.

Last night Stacey had a
party. When we were
leaving to get in a cab,
Clinton was so drunk
and stoned he fell down
her front stairs. She was
cool about it and let him
stay over to sleep it off.

Clinton's trying to fix
the bike with second
hand parts he bought
at a garage in Byron.
The guy said it would
have cost three times
as much if he had got
them to do the work.
But the thing that I'm
wondering is how can
he fix it if he doesn't
know what's wrong?

It's our second break of the shift.
The onion man is at the vending
machine dropping a quarter into
the slot. The machine won't take
his coin, and it falls with an echo
into the return cup. I reach into
my pocket, pull out an old coin,
hold it out to him, but he refuses
to take it. —New coins won't
work, I tell him. He doesn't under-
stand me but smiles as if he does,
humouring me like a child. As I
walk away, I hear the hollow
sound of the coin falling through
the body of the vending machine.
The sound, so clear and predictable,
is almost a comfort. I wonder
when he'll decide he's had enough.
I wonder when he will give up.

———

All morning, I can't
look at my mother
because I know some-
thing she doesn't. It
makes me feel like a
bad person. It makes
me feel like God.
I see a train coming
and can't get her out
of the way in time.

———

My mom's co-workers drive
me to the therapist's office,
tell me what's gonna happen,
what to expect. I'm supposed
to tell a story about when my
mother's drinking affected
me. When didn't it? My first
memory, I'm five, watching
TV in the den. I look back for
my mother. She isn't in her
yellow chair. In the ashtray,
a cigarette burns, but I won't
touch it because I'm not
allowed to play with things
that make fire. I find her in
bed, passed out. Even though
I shake her, pinch her, she
won't wake up. When I lift
her lids, her eyes roll back in
her head—wet white marbles;
and this is what I think it
looks like when you're blind.

—

I don't believe in interventions.
I don't believe in AA. It's like
recycling; it makes you feel a
little better, but it doesn't change
a thing—the world is still
drowning in plastic, and given
a chance, she will drink again.

The therapist's office is small. There's a couch, four chairs, and a large wingback in the middle of the room, which I'm guessing is where my mother will sit—like a circus act. There are two other people here from her office who I have never seen before, but they know me. They say, they remember me from when I was little. After we introduce ourselves, we sit in silence, waiting for her to arrive. They don't understand I have to live with her after this. They can go home, feeling good they've done the right thing. Not me. I secretly think it will be funny if she doesn't show. The therapist says it's important to take her off guard so she can't lie her way out of it or put up defences. She's not a textbook. I know her; she's not gonna lie because lying here and now would just make her look bad. She'll do whatever they say because it's what they want to hear. She's not stupid. Just like everyone else, even the therapist wants to feel important. She asks if I want to come back for counselling next week to debrief. I tell her I will, even though I have no intention of it. My mother walks in dressed nicely in a black skirt, nylons, a white button-down, and a gold necklace I clasped on for her this morning, my hands shaking because the clasp was so small. I can tell she just applied a fresh coat of beige lipstick. Her makeup is perfect, and her patent leather purse matches her shoes. I can tell she doesn't know why she's been asked to come here, but she senses something is up when she looks around and sees me.

—

After the intervention, the therapist
wants us all to leave so she can talk
to my mother alone. I didn't picture
it ending this way. I thought we
would leave together. It's going to
be really awkward when she gets
home. She's done something wrong
and now everyone knows it. As I
leave the room, I see my mother
cry for the first time in my life. She
tells me she loves me. I'm not sure
if it's just for show or if she means it.

———

I watch a black cat get hit
by a car. It runs right over
to me and dies at my feet.
If I were superstitious, I'd
think it might be an omen.

Clinton's cancelled
the trip to BC—for
now. He thinks we
should move out,
get a place in town
so I can finish high
school. I'm not sure
this is such a good
idea. I don't say no,
but I don't say yes
either. To save for
first and last, he's
working two weeks
straight. There's no
way I'm doing that.

Stacey and I are visiting her new boyfriend
who's in jail for stealing cars. We take the
Whiteoaks bus all the way to Exeter Road.
On the way, we pass rows of brown and
beige townhouses that look as alike
as matchsticks in a box. At the jail,
we get frisked and go through an X-ray
machine. I sit beside her in the visitor's
room while she talks on the phone through
bulletproof glass. Her boyfriend is really
cute; he's preppy, not like a criminal at all.
This is the third time he's been caught this
year. He can't seem to stop stealing cars
or doing B&Es. On the bus home, I tell
Stacey Clinton and I might be moving in
together to see what she thinks. Although
she says she likes him, Stacey doesn't think
I should trust Clinton because she says he's
the type of guy that'll fuck around on me.

The last time Clinton came
for dinner, he was rude to
my grandmother, and she
noticed. —He used to help
me up the front stairs, she
said. He used to help your
mother with all the dishes.

My mother's going to a treatment centre in Guelph. The Homewood. Apparently Gordon Lightfoot went there. It means I'll have the house to myself for a month. Whenever she comes back from these things, she's always the same. She acts all holier than thou until she starts drinking.

Each time my grandmother
visits the LPH she says it's
harder for her to get away.
So hard, that for a long time
now she's wanted both her
and my grandfather to die.
But last night she had a
dream of my grandfather
and her at a gathering with
friends. He had on a white
shirt, He was all dressed up
—and he was laughing and
joking. She says she had
long ago forgotten what he
looked like healthy. When
she woke up, she felt almost
different, almost happy.

———

Clinton and I are looking at an apartment
on top of what used to be a hardware store.
The store reminds me of my grandfather
and the place he worked in after they sold
the farm. When he smoked unfiltered
cigarettes in the storage room and washed
with lemon juice to remove the stains
from his hands. The apartment is clean
but small. So small, my mother would say,
you couldn't swing a cat. This is the type
of place I imagine the onion man lived
with his wife when they moved here. For
them the city was new and probably
seemed bigger than it was, like when you're
little and think alleys are paths to exciting
places until one day you realize they're just
spaces people park cars. As we leave,
Clinton shakes the landlord's hand in a way
I know he wants to take the place. Where
am I going to put all my stuff? The owners
have taped paper to the windows of the hard-
ware store. If I look closely, I can see the
yellow hook board where they hung the tools.

Tonight the
onion man was
walking around
in the stacks
when he should
have been on
the opposite
end of the
warehouse. He
came around the
corner while I
was taking a nap.
He startled me,
and when I woke
up unexpectedly—
I startled him.

I get a call from a girl claiming
to be Clinton's girlfriend, who
says she met him at Ace Arcade.
Clinton's sitting at my kitchen
table eating a grilled cheese
sandwich I just made him. She
asks if I'm "going" with him. I
say, —Ask him yourself and
hand Clinton the phone. My
first thought—What if I get VD?
What if I get AIDS? When he
hangs up, I ask, —Who the fuck is
that? He says—some crazy bitch
from public school who's liked
him since grade three. I don't
bother to ask any more questions
because we both know he's lying.

My mother
thinks I'm
clinically
depressed
because I'm
sleeping too
long and I'm
irritable. She
likes to have
a term for
every little
thing because
it gives her the
illusion it's a
problem that
can be fixed.

———

In all,
the world
is just
really
sad and
lonely.

When I tell Clinton I'm not moving
in with him, he says, —Yeah you are.
This starts a fight, and I lock myself
inside the bathroom. —You cheated
on me, I say through the door, and
he kicks it with his motorcycle boot
as hard as he can until I open it. The
wood by the doorknob is cracked.
What am I gonna tell my mother?
He says he did it because he thought
I was going to kill myself. I ask him
why he would think that —Because
we're just not getting along anymore.

Now that we've broken up,
Clinton says I have to get
my own way to the factory.
Sometimes my mom drives
me and sometimes I have
to take the bus. The forklift
drivers are now giving me
the cold shoulder. They're
taking Clinton's side, even
though I've done nothing
wrong. The only people
talking to me are Brenda
and Clinton's mom. Tony
was nice, but now he's not.

———

Stacey says, for her parents, she was a
mistake. The condom broke, and she's
glad her mother didn't have an abortion.
But I don't want to be here. If given the
choice, and I think we should be given
a choice, I would have opted for no,
don't bother. They say they wanted me,
but they've never really acted like it.

Today I'm trying something new.
Before we eat our lunches, I smile
and lift up my can of ginger ale in
a toast to the onion man, in solidarity.
No one talks to me anymore either.
He pauses, picks up his cola, and
toasts me back. Then he opens his
lunch box, and begins to peel his
onion. I wonder, if he'd been given
a choice, what he would opt for.

I've just finished
having a smoke
when the onion
man stops me on
my way back to
work. He holds
out a picture of
a guy that looks
like a younger
version of him.
His son. He is
cute, and he
looks like he
might be about
my age. If he
wasn't dead,
I'd go for him.

My mother and I told my
grandmother about the
treatment centre. We both
thought she would be critical;
we both thought she'd cry.
But she didn't. She just said,
—I see, as if she had just been
given a weather report. I guess
when you're eighty nothing
surprises, nothing is news.

I didn't think that it was
possible to get to the
top of the stacks with-
out a lift. It's not that
we don't know why he
did it, but why did he
do it at the factory? I
don't blame him. He
was mourning the loss
of his son. And people
here treated him badly.
Cruelness reminiscent
of a schoolyard is the
only way to describe it.
I don't know why people
like to kick someone
who is down, but they
do. Maybe it makes them
feel better about them-
selves. I looked at him
then looked away. I don't
remember seeing blood.

When Clinton found out he
came to find me and hugged
me really hard like he knew
I would want him to, and I did.
When they sent us home, he
left without saying goodbye.
I got a ride from Brenda.

No one
from the
factory
went to
the funeral.
I hope
someone
sent his
wife
flowers.

I dream the onion man,
his blood spreading out
before me, a bouquet
of flowers. My mother
says I have symptoms
of post-traumatic stress.

Clinton, me, his mom, and
Brenda are sitting outside
on the picnic tables before
our shift. It's the last day of
corn season at the factory.
I drove in with Clinton's
mom and Clinton rode in on
his bike, which he tells his
mom is now all fixed. He's
still not speaking to me, but
he sort of talks through me.
—How much money would
you take to clean up someone
else's blood? Clinton says
he'd take a thousand. Brenda
doesn't know, and Clinton's
mom says she wouldn't take
anything less than five. But I
wouldn't do it. I wouldn't do it
for any money in the world.
Clinton says, —That's because
she's lazy, and everyone laughs.

———

I saw Steve at Call the Office. He's leaving
London and going to university in the States.
I told him congratulations but didn't mean it.

I'm starting to realize no one is
happy and happiness is not a
thing to expect out of life. No
matter what they do, it seems
like no one likes their jobs.
Clinton says, —Since when do
people have to like their jobs or
be happy? —I want to be happy,
I say. —Don't be disappointed
because likely you won't. You'll
have a job you hate, raise kids
you resent, and then die. That's
just the way it is. —Maybe if
you go to university things
turn out different, I say. —You
think people who go to university
like their jobs any better? he says.
Life is depressing. That's why
it's a good idea to be drunk
for most of it or at least stoned.

Clinton and I are at the back of Scott's
Corner drinking pints of Canadian. It's
Karaoke night. It's Labour Day weekend.
Clinton is wearing a Joy Division T-shirt,
faded black jeans, Converse. I'm wearing
a flower-print dress, black shoes with
thick soles I can hardly walk in. My chest
is tight from the humidity. I have allergies.
I have anxiety. I say to Clinton, —I'm
never going to meet anyone. I'm going
to be alone for the rest of my life. Clinton
says, —Mark P. wants to fuck you. I ask
him if he's just saying that to make me
feel better. —Mark P. is a nice guy, but
I know you won't go for him, he says,
less like a comment and more like a
command. —I'm just telling you this so
that when you're lonely, you'll know
someone else is out there who likes you.

—

The Karaoke host is wearing
a grey suit. A cheap one. The
kind you get for a wedding
or funeral. He calls up a group
of secretaries who have signed
up to sing: "I Got You Babe."
They're tipsy. There's five
of them. Wrinkles have formed
around their eyes despite their
best efforts to conceal them.
We watch the secretaries sing
two more songs. Clinton doesn't
look at or talk to me. When I ask
him why he's not talking, he says
there's nothing to say. When I
ask if we are going to be friends,
he says, he's moving to BC
and when I ask him why we
can't be friends when he's in
Vancouver, he says he doesn't
know. —Won't you care how I'm
doing in school? I ask. —No, I
won't care how you are doing
in school because I hate school.
Clinton lights a cigarette, takes
a drag. —You know what I said
about Mark P.? —Yeah, I say.
—I lied, he says. I just said it
to make you feel better. —Why
would you do that? I ask. —I
felt sorry for you, he says, but
now I don't; now I think you're
a bitch. When I get up to leave,
he grabs my arm tightly. —Don't,
he says. I'm sorry. It's our last
night. Let's try and get along.

Everyone claps for the secretaries. They smile
and bow. A middle-aged man yells, Encore.
—Don't you think it's funny to watch people
make fools out of themselves, I say. —No,
he says, it's sad. —You don't like me anymore,
I say. —Not really. You broke my heart, Clinton
says. —But you cheated on me, I say. I had no
intention of marrying my dad, I say. —I'm not
like your dad. —A cheater is a cheater. It means
you have no morals. You could give someone
AIDS. —You don't have AIDS, he says.
—Sometimes it takes ten years to come out.
We could both be sitting here with AIDS right
now and not know it. —Then we'd have to stick
together forever, he says. —Why? I ask.
—Because nobody would want to fuck us. We'd
be poison. —That's all you care about is fucking
people? I say. I'm talking about dying of an
incurable disease, and you're worried about
who's gonna fuck you. I shake my head. —You
know who I bet would want to fuck you if you
had AIDS? I say. —Who? he asks. —Mark P.,
I say. Clinton grins. —There he is, he says.
He must've just gotten off work. —What's he
do, I ask? —He's a cook, Clinton says. He works
in the kitchen. —I'm gonna tell him what you said.
Clinton says, —Don't you dare or I'll kill you.

Our last stop for the night—the London
Chinese Café. We've come here almost
every day after school for the past three
years. Now Clinton's going to BC,
and I'm finishing up grade thirteen. I'm
scared to go into the future. When I look
at Clinton and I think about going to
BC with him, I know exactly what will
happen, and it won't be good. We'll end
up like his parents or mine. We'll have
kids and we'll hurt them. We'll want to
kill ourselves or we'll want to kill each
other. I'm scared to go into the future
because I don't know what will happen.
The future is like walking into a river and
not knowing if you will step on leeches
or sand. It's like going to the London
Chinese Café after school—some days
Wanda's nice, but mostly she isn't. And
the whole time you're there—even
if you're having a good time—you're
worried, at any moment, you'll say the
wrong thing and the skinheads sitting
in the booth behind you will pounce.

128 Onion Man

Acknowledgements

I would like to thank my husband, David Poolman, for the cover art and for reading endless versions of *Onion Man*. I would like to thank my friends and family for their support—especially my mother, Joyce Mockler; my sister, Susan Mockler; and my grandparents, Helen and Jim Jeffrey.

I would like to thank Shirarose Wilensky for her editorial feedback, Karen Correia Da Silva for the cover design, Heather Wood and Halli Villegas for publishing this book, and everyone at Tightrope who contributed to *Onion Man*.

Poems from *Onion Man* were published in the following journals: *The Fiddlehead, Misunderstandings Magazine*, and *Carte Blanche*. I would like to thank the editors of these publications as well as the 2010 CBC Literary Awards for selecting an excerpt of *Onion Man* as a poetry finalist, The League of Canadian Poets for selecting an excerpt for second place in their Chapbook Competition, and The Ontario Arts Council's Writers' Works-in-Progress Program for funding this project in its early stages.

This manuscript first began when I was completing my MFA at the University of British Columbia. Thanks to the faculty, students, and staff of the UBC Creative Writing Program, and George McWhirter who first worked on these poems with me. Thanks to the Banff Centre for the Arts, the Sage Hill Writing Experience, and the Djerassi Resident Artist Program where I attended writing residencies.

The following people read excerpts or drafts of this project at various stages, and I would like to express my gratitude to them: David Poolman, Susan Mockler, Michael V. Smith, Sharon McCartney, Michael Turner, Kelli Deeth, Tanya Chapman, Rick Maddocks, Wendy Wilson, Susan Braley, Roy Geiger, and Edna Alford.

Kathryn Mockler 129

About the Author

Kathryn Mockler teaches poetry and screenwriting at
the University of Western Ontario and is the co-editor
of online journal *The Rusty Toque*. She received her
MFA in creative writing from the University of British
Columbia and her BA in Honours English and Creative
Writing from Concordia University. Her writing has
been published in *Joyland*, *Descant*, *Rattle Poetry*, *The
Puritan*, *La Petite Zine*, *This Magazine*, *Geist*, and *subTer-
rain*. Her films have been broadcast on TMN, Movieola,
and Bravo and have screened at numerous festivals.
Originally from London, Ontario, she now resides in
Toronto.